THE LIFE AND TIMES OF

FIDEL CASTRO

Esther Selsdon

CHELSEA HOUSE PUBLISHERS

Philadelphia

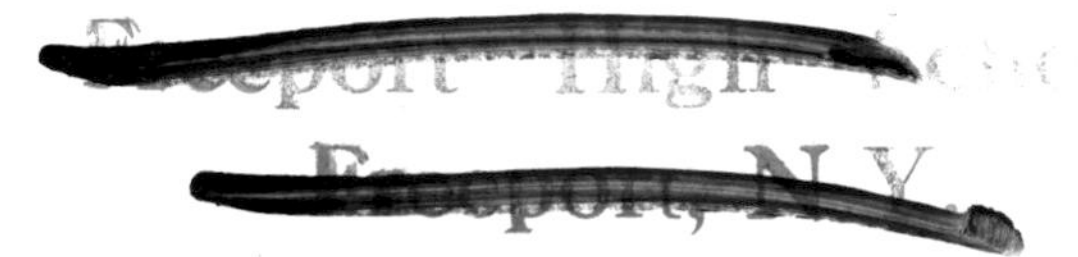

First published in traditional hardback edition

Printed in Hong Kong

Unit 13–17, Avonbridge Trading Estate, Atlantic Road
Avonmouth, Bristol, England BS11 9QD

Illustrations courtesy of Rex Features; Associated Press

Library of Congress Cataloging-in-Publication Data
Selsdon, Esther.
The life & times of Fidel Castro / by Esther Selsdon.
p. cm.
Includes index.
Summary: An account of the life and times of the man who has been the leader of Cuba since 1959.
ISBN 0-7910-4636-2
1. Castro, Fidel, 1927- —Juvenile literature. 2. Cuba—History—1933-1959—Juvenile literature. 3. Cuba—History—1959—Juvenile literature. 4. Revolutionaries—Cuba—Biography—Juvenile literature. 5. Heads of state—Cuba—Biography—Juvenile literature. [1.Castro, Fidel, 1927- 2. Heads of state. 3. Revolutionaries.] I. Title.
F1788.22.C3S45 1997
972.9106'4—dc21 97-25398
CIP
AC

CONTENTS

Castro as a young rebel leader

CHILDHOOD AND FORMATIVE YEARS

Fidel Alejandro Castro Ruz was the son of Angel Castro y Argiz, an émigré to Cuba from his native village in Galicia in the poorest, northwestern corner of Spain. Angel left Spain as a destitute thirteen-year-old orphan, intent on joining a distant relative who had settled on the faraway paradise island of Cuba. Although Fidel likes to claim that his father came to the island as a revolutionary soldier in the original wars of independence, no other member of the family ever appears to have heard this particular legend.

The uncle with whom Angel went to live, in the central Cuban town of Santa Clara, ran a brick-making business. An ambitious youngster determined to try his luck on his own, Angel worked in the factory for a while before moving to Oriente, which was at that time the prime area on the island for American investment. Signs of this economic invasion proliferated, and by the time Fidel was born the United States owned 80 percent of all sugar production concerns in the area, as well as all the local railways and the electrical firms. The newly arrived Angel at first worked on a railway being laid by the American United Fruit Company before he set up his own business as a traveling peddler. Every morning he would walk around the cane fields and sell lemonade to the workers, touting his wares on a donkey cart up and down the staggeringly beautiful countryside. He also taught himself to read and write.

By 1910 Angel had begun to use the money from his business to lease land from the United Fruit Company. He became a *colono* and grew sugar cane, which he sold to the company's mills—a practice that the corporation encouraged. He started employing farm workers to plant cane for him, and little by little he came to be known as Don Angel Castro, an affluent landowner. It was at about this time that Angel married his first wife, Maria Argota. Very little is known about this woman except that the couple had two children, Pedro and Lidia. Part of the reason for this mystery may be that the marriage failed miserably. Fidel, if he ever mentions his father's first wife, is inclined to say that she died before he was born, but every other member of the Castro family insists that Angel simply deserted Maria when he met Lina Ruz Gonzalez, an illiterate but deeply religious woman who came to the Castro household to work as Maria's maid. More than twenty-five years younger than her new husband, the pair began their relationship while Maria was still in residence in the family home, which may well explain the mystery surrounding her disappearance. Angel and Lina were married long after Fidel's birth.

For his new family, Angel built a magnificent home, constructed on wooden stilts with space underneath for cattle and fowl, just as it would have been in his native Galicia. The building was later expanded to include an office, a cow barn, and later a slaughterhouse and a repair shop. Castro insists that eventually the post office and the school were the only two buildings in the entire village that didn't belong to his father, who had become the owner of a 26,000-acre domain with more than three hundred dependent families. Angel, an imposing man over six feet tall, relished his new role as emigrant Spanish autocrat and insisted on sporting a wide-brimmed hat as well as a beard. His most cherished pleasure was to sit outside on his veranda and declare holidays for his workers—days on which he distributed largesse to the piteous indigenous folk.

At 2 A.M. on August 13, 1926, Fidel was born. He claims that he was always destined to become a guerrilla fighter since he was born as night became dawn, the ideal hour for revolutions. Surprisingly superstitious about such matters, Fidel also attaches great importance to the number twenty-six, not only the year of his birth, but also his age when he launched his first antigovernment conspiracy; his revolutionary movement became known as the 26th of July Movement. He often still picks the twenty-sixth day of each month to make important speeches. Although Fidel was named after his father's best friend, a well-known millionaire, to this day the Cuban leader goes to great pains to point out that this gentleman never officially became his godfather. Fidel, in fact, was not even christened until he was six years old, which was, apparently, a much greater source of embarrassment to him as a child than his illegitimacy.

Apart from this minor setback, Fidel's infancy appears to have been very pleasant and a good deal more privileged than the average Cuban's. At the age of four, Fidel entered the public grammar school that two of his six siblings already attended. From a very early age, Fidel was unable to tolerate any form of criticism or imposition of authority. He was disruptive in the local school and the teachers were unable to control him. His parents decided to send him to Santiago, the local capital, in order to study under a highly disciplined regime led by monks. Here he engaged in activities such as riding, hunting, and shooting, and he loved to practice his aim on his father's hens. His sisters recall that Fidel organized a baseball team of which he declared himself captain, even though he was an appallingly bad player. When his team began to lose, Fidel simply disbanded the match and went home. In this respect he took after his father, who played dominoes every evening with Lina, but who, when facing imminent defeat, would hurl the pieces to the floor and end the game.

A street in old Havana

At the age of six Fidel was transferred to a private school for rich boys in Santiago, where he lived with his godparents. He hated it. He claims to have been engaged in his first serious rebellion at this time, on an occasion when his godfather tried to spank him for some minor misdemeanor. Fidel caused such a terrible fuss about this slight to his pride that he was immediately sent from the house to become a boarder at the school. Two of his brothers later joined him there as pupils. Between them the Castro kids received a school report to the effect that they were, together, the three biggest bullies that the school had ever seen; consequently they were immediately taken away. But Fidel had already learned about absolute and uncompromised stubbornness, and back home he screamed and ranted and threatened to burn down his parents' house unless they allowed him to go back. Eventually his parents could take no more, and he was allowed to return to Santiago.

Now he stayed as a boarder with a local family and he received twenty cents pocket money a week. He spent ten cents for the movies on Sundays, five cents for ice cream afterward, and five cents for a comic he bought every Tuesday. His pocket money would be cut, said his parents, if he didn't receive top grades, so he informed his teachers that he had lost his notebook. They gave him a new one, which they filled with his real grades each week. In the meantime, he had kept his old book and continued to fill it with top grades, which he then proudly showed to his parents.

By his late teens Fidel had begun to use his school vacations constructively. He had learned to drive a tractor, and he attempted to organize the sugar workers on his father's own estate to strike against their boss for higher pay and better conditions. He reprimanded his father constantly for being an exploitative capitalist, while simultaneously permitting his parents to pay for his education at one of the most expensive Jesuit colleges in Cuba.

In 1941 Fidel took an exam that would enable him to go

to Belen College, an exclusive Jesuit high school in Havana. He had turned sixteen in August and had persuaded his parents to let him attend Belen since it was regarded as the best school in the country, even though it was also the center of Cuban aristocracy and bourgeois values. Fidel had already understood where his best interests lay and when to keep his mouth shut and put his principles behind him. He was the first member of his family to have the opportunity to study in Havana and it was his first visit to the island's capital. He did not know a soul but he was determined not to let this hold him back.

Located in a residential district of Havana, Belen was the leading educational center of the establishment elite. Discipline was strict. The boys wore uniforms and attended mass each morning at 7 A.M. Although his family was rich, this did not necessarily make him acceptable to the other boys. Occasionally he was called *guajiro* (peasant), and he found it hard to make friends. He was prone to confrontational behavior and often fought viciously with other team members if a basketball referee's decision went against him. At the age of eighteen, Fidel was proclaimed Cuba's "outstanding collegiate athlete," but by this time he had moved on from sports. His favorite subject was theological history and his favorite book the Bible, with its tales of sin, punishment, and redemption.

Fidel's time at Belen—autumn 1941 to spring 1945—coincided with Fulgencio Batista's first presidency of Cuba. Batista emerged as a democratic leader, having come to power under a military coup after a period of violent political upheaval. The United States, believing that such turbulence would inevitably lead to Communist takeover of Cuba, established discreet contact with Fulgencio Batista to help run Cuba via a succession of five stooge presidents, manipulated by Batista from behind the scenes, until he was ready to run for president himself. His leadership was a crucial period for Cuba, with its first constitutional presidency and a free press. The islanders hoped that a new era had finally dawned.

Schoolgirls in Havana

Encouraging the workers

CASTRO THE REVOLUTIONARY

Enrolling in Havana University's law faculty in 1945, Castro turned immediately to politics. The situation at the university reflected the overall state of affairs in Cuba itself, though aggravated by the youth of its student participants. Political identities and loyalties were highly volatile and only the Communists did not constantly shift allegiance. Castro was not a member of any party but he was eager to create a personal reputation as rapidly as possible. The university was a dangerous place and no sensible student ever ventured around the campus without a gun. It was a self-governing institution; since neither the police nor the army were allowed to enter the grounds, it was therefore a sanctuary for any politicians or gangsters who wished to hide from the law. Fidel at this time fancied himself more intellectual than the rest of the students, and he insisted on walking around campus wearing a dark wool suit and a necktie.

During his third year at the university Castro became familiar with the writings of Marx, Engels, and Lenin. He claims to have been immediately captivated by the ideal of utopian Communism but while at the university he never mentioned any of these specific labels. The university was run by two rival gangster groups, the Socialist Revolutionary Movement and the Insurrectional Revolutionary Union. It is impossible now to tell with which of these two groups Fidel was aligned. Followers of both still appear to believe that he was in their movement rather than the other. He must have been a chameleon charmer of a young man, constantly sensing his way toward a position of power. His external political performances, however, began in 1946 before he was even twenty. Alongside the FEU president, he attended a meeting at the house of a man who was running for the post of mayor of Havana. Fidel waited patiently for his moment and, finally, when his turn came to speak, he started out by saying that he would support the candidate but only on three conditions. First, all young revolutionary leaders killed by rightist regimes should be brought back to life; second, the candidate should return all the money he had stolen from the people of Cuba; and third, history should be turned back a century. He finished his speech with the claim that "if all these conditions are met, I shall immediately sell myself as a slave to the colony into which you want to turn Cuba." Then, demonstrating the sense of theater he was to develop so acutely, he got up and marched out of the room. His political themes have not changed very much since that very first public speech, but he grew more and more accomplished at outlining them, finishing the year with his first official speech at a public meeting. His oratorial skills were so professional by this time that he made it to the front page of the local paper. He was a rising political star and he was still not yet old enough to vote.

The year 1947 was a time of definitive political commitment for Fidel. He was one of thirty-four signatories—along with the federation president and the law school president—to a declaration condemning the reelection of Grau San Martín, the country's current president. The declaration already had the distinctive Castro ring to it, pledging, "It is better to die on your feet than to live on your knees," though Castro had, in fact, appropriated this phrase from the revolutionary Mexican leader Emiliano Zapata. It was at this time that he went on a trip to a new high-security prison, and on his return he publicly chastised the administration for its inadequacies, an act that found him a subject of media attention once more.

Senator Eduardo Chibas, the voice of anti-Grau opposition, was moved by the corruption of the government to found a new political party under the slogan "Shame of Money." Fidel was a sufficiently important person in Cuban politics by this stage to be among the hundred citizens who were invited to the historic gathering on May 15, 1947, when the new party—the PPC—was officially launched. Fidel was not yet twenty-one and was the only university leader asked to attend the event. It suited Castro greatly to create the impression that he was Chibas's favorite son and would be his political successor. He campaigned hard for Chibas in 1948, though, in private, the two men resented each other. In any event, the PPC was the only party Castro ever joined before he created his own. It was a necessary means to an end.

By the end of Castro's second year at law school, he was too preoccupied with his political career to concentrate on his studies and he didn't bother to take his exams. He never went out in the evenings except to political meetings; his friends report that they never once saw Fidel at a dance, which was incredible for Havana in the 1940s. Neither, apparently, did he have any girlfriends. He spent his time writing leaders for the student newspapers, denouncing everyone he could think of, and then making speeches in which he quoted the national hero, José Marti, at every possible opportunity, knowing that this particular technique was a surefire winner.

By this stage, Castro had become one of the louder voices of popular opposition. He could not be silenced and was therefore given an ultimatum by his teachers—he must abandon his antigovernment stand or leave the university forever. In a country in which masculinity and cowardice are incompatible, Fidel had no real choice. Not to leave would have been political suicide. He still had several law exams to complete, but instead he volunteered to be among a party of radicals who would assist in an invasion of the Dominican Republic and oust its right-wing president, Rafael Trujillo Molina. Late in July Fidel was sent to the north of Oriente to receive his first experience of basic military training. The expeditionary force of about twelve hundred men all spent almost two months aboard a fleet of boats doing virtually nothing. Eventually Fidel was put in charge of his own squad until, in September, the whole campaign was called off. Soon after this the head of the most important student union was assassinated and mayhem swept Havana. The canceled boats were on their way back from Dominica and were intercepted by government troops. Everybody aboard was arrested. Rather than face such ignominy, Fidel jumped ship and swam ashore. Two days later he was once again back at the university, making antigovernment speeches. These became more and more vociferous, and by the end of the year Fidel had become the island's most promising political star.

On February 22, 1948, Manolo Castro, Fidel's most prominent rival, was shot dead in front of a movie theater, and Fidel was immediately accused of his murder. Given the political turmoil, he decided it would be wise to vanish for a while, and a new project suddenly enabled him to do so. Argentine president Juan Perón had been anxious to found an "anti-imperialist" Latin-American Students' Association and the first meeting was to be held in April in Bogota, Colombia, with Argentina paying all the expenses. Nationalism and Anti-Americanism were the common factors unifying the students, four of whom were sent from Cuba. Naturally, Fidel became the spokesman. He was arrested on the way to the airport and, with his now well-established flair for publicity, he exploited the incident, declaring that he was on a mission designed to strengthen the bonds of friendship among Latin American peoples. The judge was immediately enthused with patriotic fervor and released his prisoner, allowing him to leave the very next day. Fidel's first trip abroad thus became surrounded by additional publicity.

Fidel was named as the student emissary to meet Jorge Gaitan, the most popular man in Colombia and the leader of the Liberal party. The appointment was set for April 9 at 2 P.M., but as he was walking over to Gaitan's office there was a sudden burst of explosive activity in the streets: Gaitan had just been shot and killed in front of his own building. Colombia erupted into violent street warfare and Fidel's baptism as an active revolutionary was a bloody one. Nobody had organized these events and yet they provided Castro with a unique learning opportunity. The congress building was invaded, and fighting continued for five days. Fidel and his associates returned from Bogotá and made the front pages of the Cuban newspapers. He had been in the right place at the right time and came back to Havana better known than ever, and determined to throw himself into the election campaign on behalf of Chibas. Chibas, however, was demolished at the polls by Grau's labor minister, Prio, who was inaugurated in October 1948.

Fidel's personal life was also moving on. He had found a girlfriend, Mirta Diaz-Balart, a philosophy student and sister of his best friend. They married on October 12. His new wife's family was also from Oriente and very wealthy. Curiously, the couple went to the States for their honeymoon and incorporated a trip to New York. (It was here, apparently, that Fidel bought copies of a number of the important socialist works that were to influence him greatly, including *Das Kapital,* Karl Marx's critical study of capitalist economy.) The young couple returned to Cuba and took up residence in a dingy hotel room in downtown Havana. On September 1, 1949, Mirta gave birth to a son, whom the couple named Fidel Castro, though the baby immediately became known as Fidelito.

Castro, meanwhile, continued to study, concentrating his

attention on labor law, while political violence increased in the capital. Prio, the president, resolved to do something to stamp out the increasing violence in the city. Instead of trying to destroy his rivals, he would work with them; thus he offered all of the rebel leaders cabinet posts as long as they promised to cease rioting in the streets. Fidel was outraged. He organized a meeting at the university naming all of the corrupt individuals involved in the scam and the effect was immediate. No sooner had he finished speaking than the university was surrounded by tanks. The problem was to get him out of the building alive. He was smuggled out with difficulty and sent into hiding in New York, where he remained incognito.

Virtually nothing is known about this visit or whether Mirta went with him, but Fidel did improve his English and he used the time to prepare for his final law exams. When he was eventually able to return to his native island in September 1950, he went immediately to Havana to take his exams. He earned a degree in Law, Social Sciences, and Diplomatic Law and immediately set up his own firm that would concentrate solely on persecuted political causes. Much of the burden of this business venture fell on Mirta's shoulders. On one occasion, when Fidel was away on one of his worthy campaigns, she called Fidel's business partner in tears to say that all of their furniture had just been repossessed by bailiffs. The partner turned up at the house and somehow managed to buy the couple some new chairs and a table, but when Fidel returned home the next day, he didn't notice a thing.

By 1951 Fidel was representing thousands of poor Havanans whose homes the Prio government was planning to destroy. He was also investigating Prio's personal corruption and campaigning intensely to become a local congressman when, in August, Senator Chibas shot himself and died. Castro profited immensely from this fantastic political opportunity, choosing to stand by the bier, lead the funeral parade, and identify himself as the leader's natural successor in every way possible. It is highly likely that Castro, who was by this time a popular hero, would have won an election had there been one, but fate intervened. On March 10, 1952, Fulgencio Batista marched into the army's main barracks in Havana and, in one fell swoop, effected a rapid, bloodless, and totally successful coup d'état. The next day he moved into the palace he had left eight years earlier and he declared himself president.

Batista was so widely hated that he became the single unifying force that Cuba had needed so desperately for such a long time. President Prio fled the country and Fidel was forced to begin a new, much tougher course of action. He formed a hard-core resistance movement from among the former members of his party. At this stage, however, the Communists were still excluded since they could not accept Fidel's sole leadership. Castro's authority in his own party remained unquestioned and he ran his men along military lines. Further peaceful political debate was now out of the question. To build up his movement, Fidel claims that he traveled forty thousand miles during the fourteen months leading up to its first major military assault, the Moncada attack. He recruited twelve hundred men and spoke to each one personally. The idea of attacking this well-known barracks in Santiago was to serve two purposes—if they were successful it would be a means of capturing a large quantity of modern weapons, and at the same time it would be a major military base from which to start a revolution. He and his men studied the area in detail. They picked Sunday, July 26, 1953, as the best possible day and only six men knew of either this date or the scene of the action. As a security precaution Fidel slept at a different house each night for a whole fortnight before the attack and he carefully avoided routine actions. He was certain of success and he was absolutely convinced that the people of Cuba would rise up en masse and support him.

Almost instantly the plan began to go wrong. Despite intense preparations, many of the cars got lost on the way to the barracks and didn't meet up at the prescribed time. Fidel's car arrived, unexpectedly, at the front of the brigade, a turn of events that caused his driver to panic and hit a curb. The engine stalled, the soldiers in the barracks were alerted, and bullets began to whiz past Fidel as, at that precise second, all the alarm bells in the building went off at once. The entire assault was over in less than half an hour. Only three men actually succeeded in entering the fort but they were immediately separated and got lost. Four men were killed and Fidel knew that there was no more he could do. He stood in the street shouting encouragement but he had no alternative. With his surviving rebels, he retreated wounded; by noon he had left for the mountains to resume the war, only this time as a guerrilla chieftain.

Castro prepared for revolution in the Sierra Maestra

The leader of "a revolution by the people"

REVOLUTION

On July 29 Raul Castro was arrested. A local identified him as the brother of Fidel and he was therefore transferred to Moncada barracks that same afternoon, certain that he would be shot. On August 1 a sixteen-man Rural Guard squad came across Fidel and his companions sleeping in a hut in a field. They were arrested and Fidel learned an important lesson—never sleep indoors. Thereafter, during nearly two years in the Sierra Maestra, even in torrential rain, Fidel always ordered his men to sleep in hammocks in the trees. But at this early stage, from the moment he arrived in the Santiago jail, Fidel was a number one celebrity. The commander of the prison proudly had a group photograph taken and Fidel was more like the guest of honor than a prisoner. Newspapers reported his arrest widely and, asked to explain himself on radio, Castro seized the opportunity to make a long speech about his ideals for his native country. All the prisoners were then transferred to the Boniato prison and Fidel spent all his time organizing and educating his men. He was in high spirits. Though held in solitary confinement, he had become the undisputed leader of the antidictator movement and he was already planning his next move.

His trial began in September 1953 with 122 defendants and 22 lawyers. It was evident from the start that the prosecutor had decided to perform his official function, but no more than that. The judge was clearly on Fidel's side and Fidel acted as his own attorney. When asked who laid claim to be the intellectual author of the revolt, Castro knew exactly how to milk the moment and solemnly answered, "The only intellectual author is José Marti, the apostle of our independence." One by one he encouraged the prisoners to stun the courtroom with horror tales about government soldiers administering beatings, accompanied by torture and brutality. The Batista regime decided things were getting out of hand. They would not allow Fidel to appear in court. Through a network of sympathizers, Fidel had a letter handed out of prison, passed to the judge, and read aloud in open court. He was not ill, it said, merely prevented from attending. He demanded to see a doctor and prove his perfect state of health; the three judges immediately cooperated, but still Fidel was not allowed out of prison. His trial was separated from that of the other men and he was transferred to an even remoter cell. Eventually, in October, Fidel was sentenced to fifteen years in jail, resulting, by the end of 1953, in his being chosen by the leading Havana weekly as one of the twelve most outstanding world figures of the year. He was transferred to the Isle of Pines prison and there, at last, the real Rebel Army was born. Once again united with his companions, Fidel spent his time organizing the troops and preparing them for battle while instilling them with lessons on philosophy, world history, and political economy.

On July 17, 1954, while still in prison, Fidel heard on the radio that his wife had been employed by the Interior Ministry and was in the pay of the government. He was staggered. He wrote to her immediately, telling her to sue for libel, but he was wrong. His sister informed him that Mirta had been working for the Ministry for a year now and, more crushingly still, she was demanding a divorce. The following year she married a government official and the pair immediately left for the United States. Fidel never saw her again; she now lives in Spain.

In the meantime, Fidel had become well established as Cuba's most famous political prisoner. In August Raul Castro was given permission to join Fidel in his cell. When asked years later in a television interview whether he ever listened to his brother's speeches in their entirety, Raul replied that his time in prison had sufficed for a lifetime already. "You know, when I was moved into Fidel's prison cell, when we were serving our sentences for the Moncada barracks assault, he didn't let me sleep for weeks. He just talked day and night, day and night."

Batista was elected president of Cuba unopposed in November 1954, but by May 1955 an amnesty bill for political prisoners was approved "in honor of Mother's day." On Sunday May 15, 1955, Fidel and all of his companions were freed. And Fidel came out fighting. Over three hundred supporters showed up to greet the liberation fighters and Fidel officially launched the 26th of July Movement on that day. Violence once more exploded in Havana, and by July the capital had become a dangerous place to live. Fidel made secret preparations to leave for the mainland, and shortly afterward he arrived in exile in Mexico with the specific purpose of training a guerrilla force to depose Batista. July 1955 was a highly significant month for Castro—he met the legendary revolutionary Ernesto Che Guevara in Mexico City, in Che's wife's flat. The two men hit it off immediately and talked for hours on end, planning their revolution and the ways in which they would change Latin America into a series of utopian, egalitarian states. Castro followed up this meeting by going on a six-week fund-raising tour of the United States and by setting up a network of rebel groups there, in Mexico, and in Cuba itself.

Serious money began arriving to fund the revolution in 1956 and Fidel gathered a team of trainee rebels in a camp outside Mexico City, where he would mold them into an ideal army. His men were rigidly controlled. They were not allowed to establish outside friendships, they could not go

Castro first met Che Guevara in 1955

out of the camp except with a companion, they were not allowed to date women or to drink alcohol, and they were forced to take turns on a rotation system, cooking and cleaning and ironing the military uniforms. Free time was used for study and lectures on revolutionary themes and the soldiers were forced to march endlessly around Mexico City and to row on Chapultepec Lake, after which they were taught to fire .30 caliber rifles with telescopic sights.

Late in September, the rebels were almost ready. They purchased a yacht called the *Granma* and Cuban leaders began patrolling the coastline in earnest. By November the plan was complete. The crossing lasted seven days in absolutely terrifying weather conditions. Che Guevara wrote that the entire boat had a ridiculously tragic aspect, with most of the men vomiting continuously. Naturally he and Fidel were the only two who weren't sick. At dawn on December 2, the yacht hit a mud tide about a mile south of the intended landing spot and the men had to jump ashore, carrying only their personal weapons. As Che later pointed out, this was more of a shipwreck than a landing.

They had found themselves in a mangrove swamp, up to their knees in water. Emerging from the swamp, the rebels came across the shack of an illiterate peasant named Angel Perez Rosabal. Castro strode up to him and declared, "Have no fear, I am Fidel Castro and we have come to liberate the Cuban people." Rosabal, who had never heard of Castro, looked on in astonishment. Fidel ordered a forced march into the hills with the lucky Rosabal as guide. Sensibly, Angel did not refuse. Spending their first night in a wooded hilltop shelter, Fidel claimed total victory. The army was at the very beginning of a twenty-five month war.

Government forces immediately began attempts to locate the men, who marched on to the Sierra Maestra—ideal guerrilla territory. And yet without the support of the Sierra peasants, Fidel would never have survived the initial weeks. By his fourth day in Cuba Fidel and the troops had reached

Alegria del Pio; Fidel, always the optimist, was so excited by this progress that he proclaimed, "Now we have won the war . . . the days of tyranny are counted." The Batista government, on the other hand, had already announced that Fidel and Raul Castro had been slaughtered on December 5, although they knew this not to be the case. The government sent out bombers to locate and destroy the rebels and they began to do just that. At Alegria del Pio Fidel and his companions were trapped inside a cane field. There were eighty-two fighters at this stage and they advanced slowly, begging food from the local peasants, who were either glad to give it or were terrified into supplying it. But the men were fed up and hungry. Crossing the sugarcane fields, they picked the stalks as they advanced and sucked them dry, dropping the discarded leaves onto the ground. All the Rural Guard troopers needed to do was follow the trail of scattered stalks and surround the rebel troops. But Fidel was nothing if not determined. He talked constantly, encouraging his men to lie utterly still on their backs in immense discomfort. "I shall never be taken alive by the soldiers of tyranny while I sleep," he proclaimed continually. "If I am found, I will just squeeze the trigger and die." His companions, and particularly his old bodyguard, Universo Sanchez, told him he was off his head and he should put his gun away before he did himself an injury. But Fidel, who had always seen himself as a grand-style leader of people, went into a sulk and wouldn't put down his gun. He was incapable of silence and kept up a continual barrage of revolutionary speech almost the entire time the men were locked into the field. He never failed in his absolute blind faith in himself and in his own powers of leadership.

Even stuck in a field, on his back, with a few more or less unarmed and hungry companions, he was already making incredibly specific plans for the ruling of his native land. And because he was so confident, his men believed that what he said was true and they took heart. As the Rural

Guard located the men and began to fire, Fidel just kept on shouting instructions. Che was wounded and the team routed but their leader would not admit defeat. Several men had to be employed to drag Fidel away forcibly from the scene of total disaster. The Rebel Army was, temporarily, suffering a major setback.

But by December 13, Castro and his companions had arrived at the house of two peasant brothers who belonged to the support network. Finally they had made the necessary contact with their organization and had a center from which to grow. More and more of the dispersed soldiers were located by peasants and brought to the brothers' house, which was established as the official base of the enterprise. Arms were found, troops regathered, and by January 1957 the reconvened force was on the move once more. On January 17, at a place called La Plata, the men located an army company and the combat was brief. Fidel was victorious and the booty fantastic. For the first time ever, Fidel had more weapons than men. La Plata was an important psychological and military milestone. By the end of February, Fidel and his men were hardened fighters, with beards and filthy clothes.

On February 16 Fidel encountered the woman who was to become the most important person in his life. Celia Sanchez Manduley was thirty-six, unmarried, and extremely intelligent. The two met in the middle of a pasture field and the moment marked a twenty-three year union, lasting until Celia's death. She was wholly dedicated to the 26th of July Movement and knew everyone who mattered in politics. She brought with her a *New York Times* reporter named Matthews, who, overcome by the romanticism of the encounter, wrote to the world that "the personality of the man is overpowering . . . a man of ideals, of courage and of remarkable qualities of leadership."

The impact was immense. Castro was immediately elevated to world heroic status. More money came flooding in to support the next three months of military expansion and hardship. This became the most bitter phase of the war. The army could not destroy the guerrillas but Fidel was too weak to venture out of the hills. More peasants joined up; more minor battles were fought; very little progress was made. The Rebel Army went on consolidating its control of the Sierra Maestra while Che was promoted to *comandante* and headed up his own small garrison. He set up an armory and a newspaper for his men.

On March 10, 1958, Raul Castro left with sixty-five men to set up a new front in the Sierra Cristal. Gradually the army was being transformed into a more professional and better-equipped force. By April Fidel had acquired a brand new jeep and the rebels held enough territory for him to be able to ride around his land like a real ruler of people. Morale was growing. A hospital was established and, in July, Castro defeated a whole battalion of men led by Major Quevedo, a former fellow student of his at the university. This was a symbolic moment for both of them. By mid-September Fidel had moved out of his mountain haven and initiated an offensive to capture the rest of Oriente. The country was in a state of collapse and now, at last, Fidel's dream began to be realized. The government recognized that they were in an untenable position and, by January, the junta in Havana had collapsed. For three days the country had no official government. But there had been no violence—it was a genuine revolution of the people. Fidel and his entourage entered Santiago on January 2, 1959, surrounded by an explosion of popular happiness. Fidel declared Santiago to be the provisional capital of Cuba and himself to be the chief of the victorious revolution. The people were ecstatic. Symbolically, the first thing Fidel did was to take control of the once-disastrous Moncada barracks and, from his erstwhile scene of failure, make a broadcast: "This is the Revolution," he said. "This Revolution was won by the People."

Castro seized power in January 1959

Fidel Castro

POWER

Castro set out to destroy every vestige of the old social order. He accomplished this by operating for well over a year on a secret pact with the "old" Communists and by entering into secret negotiations with the Soviets. The members of the Rebel Army, much as they had been essential to the first part of Fidel's plan, were not suitable for ministerial posts and so Castro unceremoniously dumped most of them fairly quickly. He had to build up his military and political controls in order to cope with any domestic opposition. He had the country ruled by a puppet leader, which enabled him to carry out his own plans for domestic reform more efficiently and from behind the scenes. He set up Marxist education camps and agrarian law reforms. His most overwhelming problem, however, was the increasing hostility of the United States, just ninety miles away. He faced this problem head on, and in April he began a tour of the United States as an exercise in public relations. He enjoyed red-carpet treatment in Washington and had a two-hour meeting with Vice President Nixon, but it was also here that he publicly ruled out democratic elections in Cuba in the foreseeable future. He went on to New York, where he was a massive popular hit, addressing a nighttime crowd of thirty thousand in Central Park.

Returning to Havana on May 7, Fidel launched the next phase of the revolution. He convened a rally of tens of

Castro befriended Nikita Khrushchev and the Soviet Union

thousands in the vast civic square and he announced on television that Cuba was beginning a new social era. Private land ownership would be abolished and the regime would be supported by arms from the Soviet Union. Castro, feeling a little more secure politically now, removed his puppet president and took over himself.

By this stage, Fidel had nationalized $850 million worth of United States property in Cuba. The Eisenhower administration, deeply irritated by this financial blow, deprived the Cubans of their vital quota in the American sugar market. This retaliatory blow pushed Fidel closer and closer to the Soviet Union, and by September 1960 he and Soviet leader Nikita Khrushchev were buddies, embracing firmly in a Harlem hotel at which they were staying as guests of the 1960 session of the United Nations General Assembly, marking the twenty-fifth anniversary of its foundation. Here the Cubans formed an important trade agreement with the Soviet Union, and the Soviets agreed to buy all the Cuban sugar that the Americans no longer wanted. On March 4 a Cuban ship blew up in Havana harbor and most locals believed the CIA was behind the bomb. Eighty-one Cubans died and, although no proof of sabotage was ever produced, Castro denounced the United States firmly. He delivered an immensely emotional speech at the funeral to overwhelming popular support, and for most Cubans the explosion confirmed Castro's constant predictions that the United States was determined to wipe out their revolution.

It was an election year in the States and President Eisenhower approved a basic policy of covert action with the CIA since an anti-Communist stance was bound to be a vote getter. Vice President Nixon, believing that he was dealing with a fully fledged Communist, developed what had been a small-scale concept into a full-scale invasion plan. By August attitudes had hardened and the Cuban cabinet passed a law of complete industrial nationalization, signaling an almost total break with the States since it was almost entirely their industries that were being nationalized. By October Castro had ordered the expropriation of 382 large industrial and commercial companies belonging to the Cuban bourgeoisie as well as every single bank on the island. He went on television to outline the rest of his economic and social program and to say that the revolution had now entered a new stage—Cubans would have to be prepared for the troops of Yankee imperialism to invade at any second. Fidel did not, apparently, realize that these troops would now be led not by Eisenhower but by the new president-elect, John F. Kennedy.

Eisenhower's farewell gesture as leader of the United States was to break off diplomatic relations with Cuba. It was not a secret by now that a CIA-led invasion of the island was being prepared. On April 12 President Kennedy offered assurances that United States forces would not intervene in Cuba; strictly speaking this was true, since the force was in fact comprised entirely of disgruntled Cuban exiles. This invasion was to become known as the Bay of Pigs fiasco. The prime favorable aspect of the plan, as far as the United States was concerned, was that there were now hundreds of Cuban political defectors in the States, all of whom wanted to overthrow Castro. The CIA, under Richard Bissell, had trained them as a crack guerrilla force especially for this purpose, but due to internal fighting the deadline for organization had expired and the guerrillas waiting to be met in the mountains were located and arrested.

Simultaneously, JFK became obsessed with public opinion. Grudgingly he gave his consent to the operation but imposed conditions that meant that it could never succeed. U.S. forces were not to be involved in landing and air strikes were only to be led by Cuban pilots, who couldn't fly properly, taking off from Guatemala, which was too far away. Finally there was only one element left that could herald victory, and that was surprise. As the flotilla of seven ships prepared to set sail from Nicaragua on April 17, 1961, and all the locals and newspaper reporters turned up to see what was going on, Nicaraguan president Samoza appeared on the dock and called out loudly and repeatedly, "Bring me a couple of hairs from Castro's beard."

The first frogman swam ashore straight into a military patrol. The poorly researched landing point, the Bay of Pigs, turned out to be the construction site of a new luxury resort, and as the soldiers landed, they were greeted by a large number of cheery workmen driving tractors. In addition, the CIA had thought that the Bay of Pigs was a sandy beach, whereas in fact it was full of pebbles, and as the frogmen emerged from the waves they all hit themselves against the rocks, while several of the dinghies had their hulls gutted and sank. As the invaders emerged they were picked up one by one and arrested. The invasion was a fiasco and Castro was jubilant. He made a great show of leading groups of interested tourists around the weapon-strewn beaches and charging them money for the privilege.

Castro's victory defined his future relationship with the United States. He used the funeral of the few dead Cubans to whip up feelings against America. There is also little question that the arms used to fight back the rebels came directly from the Soviet Union. America recognized that it had seriously underestimated Castro and that the Bay of Pigs had done nothing except consolidate his regime. He would not now be overthrown. There is a still a billboard on the beach at the Bay of Pigs proclaiming, "The first imperialist defeat in America." While Castro began producing captured prisoners on television and they all publicly repented, negotiations for their release took over twenty months and eventually involved a trade-off with over $53 million worth of medicine and food.

The Cuban Missile Crisis of October 1962 was an inevitable consequence of the Bay of Pigs. In December 1961 Castro informed Cuba and the world that his new united revolutionary political party would have a Marxist-Leninist program adjusted to the precise objective conditions of Cuba.

A food line in Havana during the Missile Crisis

He chose to announce this event on a television talk show, knowing that the news would hit the United States like a bombshell. It was at this very vulnerable moment in Cuban history that Khrushchev proposed the deployment of nuclear weapons on Cuban soil.

"We preferred the risks of great tension," said Castro, "to the risks of the impotence of having to wait for a United States invasion of Cuba." Accepted wisdom on what happened next is that a nuclear war might possibly have begun if Soviet ships headed for Cuba had not halted on October 24 without crossing the quarantine line drawn up by JFK. If they had not braked themselves, they would have been forced to do so by U.S. warships and planes. By October 28 a heated exchange of letters had taken place between the superpowers and the crisis was over, but Castro never concealed his anger at the Soviet Union for having struck a deal with the United States to repatriate the missiles without consulting him first. It was this attack on his absolute control over all events concerning Cuba, always his most sensitive area, that led to his coolness toward the Soviet form of Communism for so many years to come. But Cuba needed Russia for its economic survival and so a marriage of convenience was formed. Castro made his first trip to the Soviet Union, heralding a triumphant personal success. Cuba was now, at last, secure from external attack and, in the two decades to come, Fidel would maintain the course he had already struck. Now he was to move on from the role of revolutionary leader to that of grand old dictator and world statesman.

The loyal Cuban military

LATER YEARS

The death of Che Guevara in the Bolivian jungle on October 8, 1967, had a profound effect on Fidel Castro. Che had disappeared in 1965 for reasons that have never been fully explained, after having been appointed Minister for Industry. Having always differed fundamentally with Fidel on a number of policies, Che was, undoubtedly, a much harder-line Marxist than his friend, believing that every worker should receive an identical wage whatever the nature of his or her job. Fidel considered that this could never work and yet Che's departure was a big symbolic blow to the original aims of the revolution. From that moment on his leadership would be more about economic management than revolutionary romance, but even under these terms, by 1968 the economy was approaching bankruptcy and Cuban production had ground to a halt. It was fortunate for Cuba, at least, that the Soviet Union invaded Prague at this time. The whole world was stunned by this act and Castro, being the only leader of any note who would agree to support the Kremlin at this time, was the single beneficiary of events. He established a new claim to Soviet economic support and, while his fragile economy improved only slightly, with massive bolstering from Russia Castro had more time to concentrate on becoming an important world statesman. He set off on a world tour, concentrating mainly on extending his influence

Rolling cigars in Havana

in the new independent African states and establishing a particular presence in Angola. He had the Cuban debt deferred permanently and declared that Cuban-Soviet relations were a model of true fraternity. Translated, this meant that, by the mid-1970s, Cuba was receiving over half of all Soviet foreign aid.

In 1976, Castro created a new Cuban constitution, entirely rewriting the whole political and judicial system. The constitution itself defined Cuba as a "socialist state of workers and peasants and all other manual and intellectual workers" and named the Communist party as the highest leading force of the society and of the state. It hailed José Marti as the leader of the revolution and then Castro as its guiding force and implementer. Thus enshrined in the most important legal text in the country, Castro was effectively named Leader for Life. It would now be unconstitutional to challenge him in any way. He had become the head of state as well as the head of government and total power was vested in him, with Raul as first vice president and second-in-command in every other post.

The decade between 1976 and 1986, the year in which Fidel turned sixty, was generally devoted to foreign policy and to the attempt, with notable lack of success, to improve the Cuban economy. Meanwhile, "interests sections" in Washington were formed, since ambassadorial contact was still not officially permitted and these provided much better channels for communication between the two governments. In 1979 Castro was elected chairman of the Non-Aligned Movement and he thus took on the mantle of Third World leadership to which he had long aspired. He hosted that year's conference and kept the spotlight firmly on himself. In October of the same year Fidel returned to New York for the first time in nineteen years to address the United Nations General Assembly as chairman of the Movement. He found this turn of events immensely gratifying.

Since 1985 Castro has devoted much of his time to the

problem of Third World debt and this has become the main thrust of his (increasingly lengthy) speeches. At home, however, Castro refuses to relax centralized planning or to experiment with market forces. He is now the undisputed leader of a volatile nation, one that he has led for over a third of a century. He is a grandfather in a country with the most advanced medical system in the Third World, but beyond this advance his country has not changed in years, while other Communist systems have either moved on or been abolished altogether. Since 1980 he has had few fresh ideas and he now looks like a man locked into a political time warp. He continues to rant at great length about "vile money" and declares that young people drink too much and do not have the same moral fiber as their revolutionary parents. He remains constantly furious about the high rate of absenteeism among Cuban workers and their low productivity rate. At a Communist Party congress in 1986 Fidel made a speech lasting five hours and forty minutes in which he declared that any opposition to himself was counterrevolutionary. Celia Sanchez, his only real intimate, died of cancer in 1980, and since that day Fidel Castro has remained a fervent revolutionary dictator, but one who continues to be increasingly isolated and alone.

Fidel Castro meets Mikhail Gorbarchev

INDEX

INDEX

Cuban agricultural workers